JOURNALING WORTH DOING

A Practical Guide

Unlock your intuitive wisdom and expand your female inner power, leadership and joy

by Noomi Melchior Natan

Published by: Noomi Natan Leadership Limited

ISBN: 978-1-7384551-0-2 (paperback)

ISBN: 978-1-7384551-1-9 (hardback)

ISBN: 978-1-7384551-2-6 (ebook)

Cover Design: The Cloud Digital

Cover stock photos: Norwood Themes and Blue Planet Studios

Author photo: Louise Adolphsen

Interior Design: Gigi Chik

Special thanks to the early readers and proof readers: Joanne Owen, Anja Eisenbrandt, Barbara J. Hunt, Amanda Gosling, Holly Hufnagel, Valerie Vandermeer, Mel Norman, Sorena Veerman and Gigi Chik

With gratitude to all those who made me the person I am today and everyone who helped make this book a reality.

Extra appreciation for:

My parents, mor and far, for always believing in me.

My husband, Eviatar, for his endless love and encouragement to think and act big.

To my daughters, Aluma and Emilia, who make me want to be and do better every day.

TABLE *of* CONTENTS

INTRODUCTION

A great place to start

To you

Dear wonderful woman.

You are full of wisdom, inspiration and an immense ability to impact the world around you for the better. This is true, even if you sometimes forget it and feel like you need someone else to remind you.

My intention with Journaling Worth Doing is that you remember your own power, learn how strong your intuition is and how many answers you can easily access with some guided journaling.

You will activate your self-trust and create additional space and momentum in your life.

Over the past few years journaling has become a priceless tool for me, and many of my clients, and I want to share this gift with you.

Have you noticed how wise you are when it comes to helping someone else with how to make their dreams come true? Or how clearly you can see what will help when your favourite character in a novel or a drama is struggling?

Yet, often when it comes to your own life that kind of clarity and wisdom seems harder to access. By using the Journaling Guides in this book, you will unlock that inner wisdom and connect with your natural self-coaching abilities.

This kind of journaling is nothing like the "Dear Diary entries" I wrote when I got my first journal at the age of 13. Although those were cathartic, they were mainly a lot of descriptions of whatever I had done that day, what was happening in the family or which boy I had a crush on.

In my later teens and well into my 20s I mainly journaled when I was upset, or I had a strong longing for something or someone. I know this as my mum recently cleared out the basement and brought me a massive bag of my old journals from Copenhagen to Oxford. I scanned a few before throwing most of them in the bin.

It is not that this kind of journaling wasn't helpful, because it definitely served a purpose, but over the last few years journaling has taken on a whole new importance for me.

All my years of coaching and doing personal growth work merged into my journaling approach. I started noticing how my journaling really became mini self-coaching sessions. The more I prioritised time for this kind of focused journaling, the better everything else flowed.

I became aware of the positive impact on my mental state and my ability to show up more as I wanted. I saw clarity arriving fast and results in all areas of my life happening in a better way.

This made journaling an invaluable tool to strengthen my personal power, my intuition and growth as a human, mother, leader, coach and business owner.

I started sharing these methods more deliberately with various clients both in one-to-one sessions and in group programs. I even decided to run monthly guided journaling sessions online for one of my programs called the Female Inner Power Club. In the first session I used the Journaling Guide that is now in this book as: When you are frustrated or bothered by something.

The week after that guided journaling session, two clients from the Female Inner Power Club spontaneously and independently of each other shared how they had used the exact journaling script three times that week for different issues and gotten a breakthrough each time. That is when I knew I needed to share this much further, and this is how the idea for this book was born.

With these Journaling Guides you will be able to coach yourself to clarity, increase your ability to lead yourself and accelerate your momentum towards whatever you want to create in your work and personal life.

How to use this book

This is not a book you just read. This is a book you use.

Dive into it as often as feels good and in a way that suits your life and personality without it feeling like a chore or something you can fall behind on.

I want you to make it work for you. Perhaps you will choose to use Journaling Worth Doing by:

- Browsing the index and selecting a Journaling Guide that fits your mood or circumstance that day
- Intuitively opening the book on a specific page, trusting that this is the exact Journaling Guide that will support you in that moment
- Going through each Journaling Guide in order, one at a time, to experience the full range of what the book has to offer

Do what feels best to you.

Over time, there will likely be guided sessions you will return to frequently and some questions will become your favourite go-to ones.

I hope that you will leave your self-coaching journaling sessions feeling more confident about navigating what is next for you, ready to act and to radiate the magic that is inside of you.

How to journal

My meditation teacher always says: "There is no such thing as a bad meditation." I would love for you to adopt the same sentiment for your self-coaching journaling sessions. There is no such thing as a bad journaling session. Sometimes the breakthroughs are instant, the nuggets obvious and the elevated feeling super strong. Other times you might continue percolating after the session or discover another layer to explore before you unlock the clarity or the shift you want.

Be generous with yourself and don't censor any thoughts. Let go of judging your words or any feelings that arise. Just write. Skip questions that don't appeal to you but pay close attention to it if you have real resistance to a question. Often where we have resistance is where we can gain the biggest breakthroughs.

I highly recommend feeling proud of yourself every time you journal, no matter how long you wrote for and no matter the outcome. You are strengthening the relationship between you and yourself, and what could be more important than that! Like any relationship there are ups and downs, and that is OK. Just keep loving yourself. Celebrate the fact that you made time to journal and tune in.

Often, I am asked if it is best to journal on paper or on a computer, if it should be in a nice notebook and if it is important to go back and read what you wrote. Guess what my answer is? Do what feels good. Make it fit for you.

There are times, when I already know before even writing a single word that I don't want to see it again. Then I might write with pen on scrap paper that I throw in the bin after. If I am in a rush, I might type my journaling in an electronic document or in a "note" on my phone and then just close it without saving it when I am done with my journaling session.

Other times, the journaling will have a different vibe and I will write in a notebook, save the document or even just summarise and copy out key pieces from the journaling, which I then store in a safe place, so I can benefit from whatever nuggets and insights that came up.

Let your intuition guide you; play with pen and paper or type in a document to see if it makes a difference to you. Perhaps there are even times where you feel like creating a ritual around the journaling and light your favourite candle. Make your journaling sessions moments where you look after yourself.

How to make time for journaling in your already very full life

Perhaps the most important question is how to even find time to journal.

My guess is that your life is full and busy. Mine is. And as much as I would delight in having hours and hours to just journal, contemplate and be, often I am squeezing in my self-coaching journaling practice between a lot of life and tasks.

I love journaling outside of the house, particularly at a nice café, where I cannot see the laundry or hear the children. But on many days, all I can fit in is 10 minutes of journaling at home, and even those 10 minutes might be interrupted by another human or perhaps by a runaway thought.

I share this to make sure you don't feel like there is a standard way or that you need to be totally focused for the self-coaching journaling to work. It is OK to get distracted. It is nice not to be disturbed, but life is life and my experience is that a little goes a really long way.

I have designed the Journaling Guides to be used in short spurts of time and in such a way that you can flex them to fit your window of time. 15-20 minutes is a delicious amount of time to move through a guided session. (Hurry to the next paragraph if that sounds like way too much time.) Depending on how long you spend on each question, you might find that you need more or less time for a Journaling Guide. Skip questions if you are running low on time, and stay longer on them when you can make time work for you.

However, if you only have 3 minutes, or if you are new to journaling and anything more than 3 minutes feels way too daunting, start with those 3 minutes. Pick a Journaling Guide and answer just one or two of the questions. Let it be easy. Let your journaling muscle build over time.

My hope is that even after following a single Journaling Guide in this book, you will know the power of self-coaching journaling and see that even though it "takes time" to journal. This kind of journaling will overall save you time, because you will have more energy, more clarity and more confidence to make better moves.

What we truly value, we will make time for. And the time dedicated to self-coaching journaling will come back to you many times over.

Making journaling into a powerful habit

If you want to stay consistent with something, make it into a habit.

I have clients that have made journaling a daily morning practise (yes, they have full-time jobs and several children). They report that a 10-minute journaling slot can power the rest of the day so much that they notice a significant difference in the quality of how they feel about themselves, their day and what they can deliver.

To inspire you to prioritise using the Journaling Guides here are just a few of the benefits my clients have reported receiving:

- Saving time and being much more productive by shifting their procrastination and overthinking super quickly
- Trusting their intuition more because the journaling clears the noise
- Increased confidence leading to the quick growth of their leadership impact
- Feeling much happier and loving their lives more
- Releasing frustration with their spouse quickly and being able to find mutually satisfying solutions
- More patient with their children and other humans too because the journaling helps to get present and grounded
- Getting a promotion / pay-rise / better business results

because they are gaining more courage to take action on what they really want

- Clarity on how to navigate tricky situations including what to say to team members and how to look after themselves in the midst of a lot of work

At the beginning, daily journaling might seem like a habit that is totally out of reach. So instead, aim for a weekly session. I love Sunday morning journaling myself, but pick any day and time of day that works for you and your life.

Choosing a specific day and time of day makes it easier to stick to and create a habit around. For example, choosing Thursday evenings at 8pm as your weekly journaling slot is a firm decision that becomes a date with yourself. You could even have a journaling partner, a great friend, where you each do your own journaling and then message each other after the session to share one insight that came from your respective sessions.

In my online program, the Female Inner Power Club, we have monthly guided journaling sessions and although we keep the journaling private - with me guiding members through the questions - the energy of being with others that are also doing their own inner work is very powerful and helps elevate the power of journaling.

Why journal? Why not just think?

Can't you just think your way to clarity and answers? Why spend time journaling?

A study published by the National Science Foundation from 2005 stated that the average human has about 12,000 - 60,000 thoughts per day, whereof 80% are negative and 95% are almost identical to the day prior. We get stuck in familiar thinking loops, and since our thoughts impact the quality of our lives and what we believe is possible, thinking the same thoughts keeps us stuck in the status quo.

In my experience it is much harder to upgrade our thoughts if we just try to think our way there. You can definitely hold questions in your mind and contemplate answers without actually writing anything down, but most of us will find our mind struggles to stay disciplined and focused after the first couple of questions. Our mind is so used to thinking in certain patterns that very quickly it will fall into a familiar thinking loop, and you will miss out on the benefit of new thoughts.

Self-coaching journaling will help you shift your emotional state, bring you back into your power, as well as clarify, renew and elevate your thinking.

Journaling examples

When I buy a recipe book I love to see photos of the finished dishes. I want to see images of how the recipe works. In a similar vein I have added a mix of modified client examples, excerpts from my own journaling and a few fictional examples. This is in no way trying to show you the "right" way of using a Journaling Guide or answering a question, but to inspire you with how it can look and work. Take what is useful and leave the rest.

Remember

I always say: Trust yourself more than you trust anyone else.

Our society teaches us to get answers from experts. Ask the doctor what to do with your health, ask your boss or mentor how to succeed with your career, and ask the internet for a conflict resolution tip when you are in a difficult situation. Except this approach is massively flawed in this case, and you already know that. How can anyone know what is right for you, better than you?

The more you use the Journaling Guides, the more confident you will be in trusting your inner wisdom.

Finally, remember to bring curiosity, self-compassion and have fun.

Let's get journaling.

Book Bonus: Sometimes a little help can be useful to transition from your active life into your journaling time. I have recorded a potent 3-minute Get Ready to Journal guided meditation to support you.

Go to www.noominatan.com/bonus to access this free 3-minute meditation.

Always trust yourself
more than you trust
anyone else

■ ■ ■

RELEASE JOURNALING

A great place to start every journaling session

The purpose of Release Journaling is to let go of anything that is on your mind without a need to structure it. Our minds are so busy with an overflow of thoughts, and Release Journaling is like opening the valve to your mind, so the clutter can start flowing out. To be able to access the wisdom in you, it is helpful first to clear out some of the noise.

You essentially just start writing down your thoughts. There is no need to make sense of anything. You write a stream of consciousness, just as you hear it in that moment. It might start like this:

Example:

> *It is time to start journaling and I don't have much time. I need to remember to organise pickup tomorrow for Sandra and buying a gift. Maybe I should do that now. No, it is my journaling time. I really want to get something out of this time and I need to focus more. I want this to be about me. There is so much to do at work and my to-do list gets longer all the time so I don't really know how I can possibly work less but it has to be possible. I am so ready for that promotion but what if I then end up working even more... I am tired. I want this, but I am tired. I can do this. I really hope I can.*

You are allowing yourself to capture all the fast-moving thoughts, and the things that are top of mind. Often it might include lots of practical things and to-do's as well as the emotions that are in the foreground. Sometimes it might be deeper and more existential.

Even if it seems like nothing productive is happening, something very important is happening when you allow yourself to write out your thoughts. You are witnessing yourself, decluttering your mind and making space inside. Even a bit of thought-clearing can make it much easier to find your calmness, clarity, self-love, inspiration and get the wisdom that is inside of you flowing.

The aim is not to hold on to these thoughts. As soon as you have written them down you let them go, and you can discard the document whenever you have finished your Release Journaling.

The key with Release Journaling is to stay neutral. Don't judge and don't make it to mean anything. Imagine you are standing a few steps away and just witnessing this stream of consciousness being captured.

Once you have done a little bit of Release Journaling you can jump into any of the other Journaling Guides. You will be able to go deeper and faster if you have done a bit of Release Journaling first.

Start your Release Journaling now.

Let's journal.

What is on your mind? Just write.

Book Bonus: Do you want to take your Release Journaling to the next level and clear out the mind chatter in a deeper way? If yes, you can use tapping – also called EFT - to clear your thoughts.

Go to www.noominatan.com/bonus to access a free 5-minute video that takes you through how to do this step by step.

THE 25 JOURNALING GUIDES

calmness & inner power

Journaling Guides 1 - 4

01

When you have very little time and want some quick clarity

Some days, time is extra tight. This guide will help you get some quick clarity in just three questions. Don't think. Write the first answers that come. You can always go back and deepen them later.

Let's journal.

What do you want more clarity on?

What is really the question you would like an answer to?

What answers do you already have?

Example:

What do you want more clarity on?

How to run the next team meeting.

What is really the question you would like an answer to?

How can the team meeting feel connecting so there is good energy, but we also agree on how to deliver the Q4 targets.

What answers do you already have?

When I am impatient and stressed meetings go less well, so I want to make sure I show up in a good state. Team meetings are also better when everyone contributes. I dislike it when it is mainly me that speaks. The questions I used for our summer session would be a great way to start the meeting. And maybe Anna can help run part of the meeting.

When you are fully present, a little time goes a long way

■ ■ ■

02

When you are frustrated or bothered by something

This Journaling Guide is a firm favourite with my clients because it can be used in so many different circumstances. Whenever you feel frustrated by something or someone these journaling questions will help you shift, reframe and come to solutions.

When we are bothered by something for more than a brief moment, it is usually because we have attached some kind of negative meaning to it, and we are predicting that something unwanted will happen next.

For example, you might be bothered by something that happened at work last Friday. You might have then made it mean that you cannot trust your colleague and you might be predicting that it is going to be a nightmare working with this colleague going forward, which means you will have to work a lot harder and with no support.

Furthermore, we end up giving our power away because we have (unconsciously) decided that this person / situation / thing is allowed to bother us. For example, if you are bothered by this work colleague who did something last Friday, you have unconsciously decided that this colleague holds power over whether you will enjoy your work and how much work you have to do on this project. We can of course argue for this to be true, but that will not help you. Notice how much power this colleague gets to hold over your work happiness if you stick with this narrative.

So instead, what can you decide? Maybe you could choose beliefs like these instead: No matter what others do; my work is always respected. Whether I am working alone or with others, breakthroughs can come at any moment. There is always support available, also from unexpected sources.

What helps shift our frustration is choosing a different and more empowering narrative. Deciding what we want to focus on and proactively choosing how we want to approach the person or situation grounds us back into our power.

Let's journal.

What are you bothered by at the moment?

What are you telling yourself that isn't helpful?

What are you predicting that isn't helpful and what negative meaning have you attached to this?

What does that tell you? (Just write and see what comes. No censoring)

So what is this really about? And what needs of yours are not being met here?

What would be more helpful to focus on?

What would be more helpful to tell yourself?

How can you bring the power back to you?

What can you decide? What is true about you regardless of this bothersome thing / person?

What is important for you to take away from all that you have just journaled?

Example:

What are you bothered by at the moment?

I am really frustrated that my mother-in-law is living with us right now.

What are you telling yourself that isn't helpful?

I can't breathe. There is no space to be alone. She might end up staying here forever. She is sucking the life out of our house.

What am I predicting that isn't helpful and what negative meaning have I attached to this?

I am predicting there is no end in sight. That it is permanent. The negative meaning is I no longer enjoy being in my home.

What does that tell me?

I am struggling to appreciate my mother-in-law. I feel like I have no say. I am only seeing the difficult sides of this situation. I have no space for empathy at the moment and I am full of judgement and frustration.

So what is this really about? And what needs of mine are not being met here?

My need to have space is not being met because my mother-in-law is sleeping in the office. And she has a huge need to talk, so she is constantly seeking me out for conversation and I just want some quietness and time where I don't have to speak to her or anyone for that matter.

What would be more helpful to focus on?

It would be more helpful to focus on how something good could come from this situation however long it might last.

What would be more helpful to tell myself?

Something good will come of this. I appreciate that my husband has a big heart and wants to support his mother. I am grateful that we have the office so she has a private room she can sleep in. That is a real luxury. Maybe I can create a new place to work or to have my quiet space while she is staying with us. And I actually think it is good for the children to learn to have empathy and respect for an elderly person.

How can you bring the power back to you?

It is in my power to choose to go into the office more often and to find other ways to get my quiet times. I can go for more walks and maybe I can put the desk in our bedroom for now.

What can you decide? What is true about you regardless of this bothersome thing / person?

I will decide that no matter how many people live in my house I can get my needs of quiet time meet. I want to be kind to others, also to my mother-in-law, and when I make sure to meet my needs first it is much easier to be the kind of woman and daughter-in-law I really want to be.

What is important for you to take away from all that you have just journaled?

I can communicate to my mother-in-law that I need some time where she doesn't ask me questions. She doesn't want to be a burden, so I hope I can say it in a kind way. But by not saying anything to her I have made myself feel so upset and that is actually not kind to all of us. This can easily get a lot better.

Being fully in your
power is the most
valuable contribution
you can make to
your surroundings

■ ■ ■

03

When you are feeling anxious and want to feel calmer

Anxiety can, depending on its intensity, be a slight energy-drain or be completely paralysing. Use this Journaling Guide when you feel strong enough to work independently on shifting some anxious thoughts.

If you are experiencing intense and ongoing anxiety you might want to seek professional 1:1 help.

A few points about anxiety that will help you get the most out of this Journaling Guide:

- We tell ourselves stories all the time. When we feel anxious, we are not telling ourselves a good-feeling story. Spotting that it is a "story", and not the truth, can help us reveal where and how our minds might be tricking us.
- As humans we are wired for survival. Fear and anxiety are strong instincts that get triggered on a basic level to keep us safe. So, although our rational selves want to let go of the anxiety, the reason we hold onto a fear is often because we are getting some hidden "safety benefit" from it. These benefits can be that we get to be taken care of, we get to protect ourselves or we get to stay small; all so we don't need to fear failing or being judged on a bigger scale.

- Our anxiety increases when we decide that things are out of our control and when we feel powerless. We cannot control what is going on around us or what others do; but what helps is noticing and deciding that we have a choice and we have power over what we want to feel, think and focus on. Calmness and feeling safe can only truly come from within and the better we get at directing our mind and body towards calming thoughts, the more we can tame our anxiety.
- Finally, I want you to remember that it isn't wrong to feel anxious. As just shared, we are wired for survival and therefore wired to be suspicious and afraid. You are perfectly imperfect just as you are. Any anxiety you might experience doesn't get to define you. You are human; a wonderful human being who is willing to do her inner work.

Let's journal.

What are you feeling anxious about?

What story (or stories) are you telling yourself that is making you anxious? About you? About other people? About the future?

What is the anxiety really about?

Why are you unwilling to let go of this story and fear? What are you getting from holding onto this story?

What do you really need?

How can you give yourself what you need now? And how can you feel what you want to feel right now?

What will help you feel calmer right now? Remember, we tell ourselves stories all the time, so how can you tell yourself a story that makes you feel calmer and also feels true. There is never just one way to tell the truth.

Example:

What are you feeling anxious about?

That the interest rates are going up and everything is getting more expensive.

What story (or stories) are you telling yourself that is making you anxious?

That we might not be able to afford our mortgage or that we will need to cut costs a lot. That we will be under massive financial pressure and that will lead to arguments and stress and all kinds of bad things.

What is the anxiety really about?

On one hand it is about financial fears and on the other it is about whether I trust myself, and us, to get better under pressure.

Why are you unwilling to let go of this story and fear? What are you getting from holding onto this story?

It seems like the sensible thing is to be afraid of the economy, though as I am writing this, that makes no sense to me. How can being afraid be a good thing. I guess I am holding onto this story because it is a story I hear all over the media and from so many people.

What do you really need?

I need to run a few worst-case scenarios but mostly I want to spend my energy on believing in good things. And I am definitely not making great decisions when I am anxious.

How can you give yourself what you need now? And how can you feel what you want to feel right now?

I can give myself space to breathe. I think I will feel better if I am grateful for what we have right now rather than being fearful of losing it.

What will help you feel calmer right now? Remember, we tell ourselves stories all the time, so how can you tell yourself a story that makes you feel calmer and also feels true. There is never just one way to tell the truth.

A better story would be that we will get creative with adding extra income streams and cutting down on expenses. There are always people that do well, no matter what the world economy is doing, and so we get to be those people.

Book Bonus: You might also want to use tapping / EFT to help you release the anxiety and increase your capacity to support yourself with any strong emotions.

Sign up to the free Book Bonus at www.noominatan.com/bonus to get instant access to a short video where you can learn this easy and powerful technique.

Tell the stories you want to live

■ ■ ■

04

When you want the most helpful advice

Have you noticed how easy it is for you to be wise, when it comes to sorting out your friends' challenges? It is quite funny, how we can easily see what others need to focus on to shift their situation. And yet, when it comes to our own stuff, we can so often feel stuck.

Let's use that wisdom you know you have when it comes to advising others, to now help yourself. This Journaling Guide will help you give yourself the most helpful advice.

The premise is this: What would you tell a great friend or a good colleague in your situation? What advice would you give them if you were speaking lovingly but completely honestly and not holding anything back?

Here are the steps:

- Access the wise friend in you and then write to yourself in third person. I promise you will not become weird by doing this. Writing to yourself in the third person will bring in some of that magic that flows much easier when you are talking to someone else you care about.

- Use the sentences below as prompts (if helpful) or free-write, or do both. The prompts are there to help you write to yourself in a powerful way. But change them to fit your narrative and make sure it feels good. Read the example for one way the letter can look.
- Give yourself that loving straight-talking advice and support.

Let's journal.

Write down these sentence-starters and complete them with your own words. Add extra sentences and modify the prompts to fit how you like to write and speak, so the language feels more like you.

Dear [YOUR NAME] I know you have been feeling challenged about….

I can see you feel stuck or frustrated with …

And it hasn't been easy because …

From a neutral perspective here is what I see ...

From a deep place of love and respect I would like to call you out on your unhelpful narrative because you keep talking about ... and saying that …

And those statements are arguing for your limitations rather than what's possible.

What I think you are afraid of is …

Here is why I know you can handle this situation … (share some of your great traits)

Focus on …

And here is what I think will be most helpful right now …

And here are some things you can do …

Example:

> *Dear Angela,*
>
> *I know you have been feeling challenged about how to do your best at work, when you are also taking your mother to cancer treatments and you are trying to keep your home life afloat right now.*
>
> *I can see you feel frustrated about how much is on your shoulders and how much you have to do.*
>
> *And it hasn't been easy because you are the main care-giver both at work in your leadership position, with your mum and to a certain extent at home in your family.*
>
> *From a neutral perspective here is what I see: I see an amazing woman who is living an intense chapter of her life. I see a wonderful friend who is giving more than is good for her and she is getting stuck into the martyr role and it is becoming unhelpful to her.*
>
> *From a deep place of love and respect I would like*

to call you out on your unhelpful narrative because you keep talking about how you have to do it all alone and I want to remind you that you have a lot of people that love you and they will help if you ask them to. Remember how your neighbour was happy to do that errand for you?

When you are telling me how much you have to do and how hard it is, you only feel the pain of this situation and that makes it all a lot harder.

If instead you choose to focus on the connection with your mum during her treatments and appreciate yourself for how you fit in being there for her, then I think you will feel a lot better.

When you are focusing on all your obligations you are adding to your exhaustion and depleting yourself more than necessary.

What I think you are afraid of is: Losing your mum. Not being enough for everyone. Being imperfect. Something falling apart while you are holding a lot in an intense chapter of your life.

Here is why I know you can handle this situation: You are so filled with love and care and you are really good at your work.

Focus on: I would love you to notice the love and many great relationships you have in your life. You can look at all the humans you are serving as obligations and as them taking energy from you. Or you can get curious about how you can deepen each of those connections. You do have time to hug your children and really be present in those hugs. You do have time to breathe deep and celebrate one of your team members for trying a new task. You do have time to be grateful for the fact that you live a full life.

And here is what I think will be most helpful right now: Focus on deepening connections. Look in the mirror and tell yourself, you are proud of yourself. Also ask for more help. There is more help available than you think. You don't need to know who to ask. Ask from a place of power rather than from a victim place and help can come.

And here are some things you can do: Do look after yourself even if you feel like there isn't time for it. The more energy you have, the quicker and easier everything else will flow. So ask yourself what you need right now and then make it happen. You are important and I know you can make space for looking after Angela's needs first and it is not nearly as time-consuming as you think.

With love from me.

No matter what is going on, now is a good time to breathe

■ ■ ■

self-love & joy

Journaling Guides 5 - 9

05

When you want to move from self-doubt to believing in yourself

This Guide is perfect for those days where you are wondering if you are good enough to do what you want.

When we are stuck in self-doubt, we cannot show up as our most powerful selves. Self-doubt also easily leads to procrastination and inaction. This means not only are we depriving ourselves of feeling great, but we are also depriving the world of the value we could potentially add, but that we are holding back, because we are unsure of ourselves.

Use the sentence prompts and questions to uncover the self-doubt and reveal the underlying fears. Then afterwards you will shift into a more powerful self that is ready to move forward.

Let's journal.

I don't feel good enough for/to …

I don't know if I am good enough for/to….

Who am I to…

Then dig deeper. What is it that you are really afraid of not being good enough at?

What if you actually succeeded at the thing you thought you weren't good enough at? What if you actually managed to do it? What do you fear might happen then?

What do you have to be willing to risk if you want to shift from self-doubt to confident action-taking? And is that risk worth it?

What if we just decided that if you truly have the desire to create / make / become something then you can absolutely do it? What would you think and feel then?

Continue with these sentence prompts:

If I now know I am good enough to… then …

If I now know that I am the right person to… then …

If I now know that other people actually really want me to … then …

What will you choose to believe about yourself and what do you want to move forward on?

What action will you now take?

Example:

> *I don't feel good enough to write a best-selling book.*
>
> *Who am I even to think that aiming for a best-seller is something I should go for.*
>
> *I don't know if I am even good enough to complete a manuscript and get it all the way to published book.*

Then dig deeper. What is it that you are really afraid of not being good enough at?

> *I am afraid that I am not enough of a completer to get a book out. And I am afraid that my thoughts aren't coherent enough to be really worthy of a book.*

What if you actually succeeded at the thing you thought you weren't good enough at? What if you actually managed to do it? What do you fear might happen then?

> *If I succeeded in publishing a book that became a best-seller even though I wasn't' good enough maybe people won't like the book and instead of it bringing more opportunities to me and my business maybe it would bring bad reviews and a negative reputation.*

What do you have to be willing to risk if you want to shift from self-doubt to confident action-taking? And is that risk worth it?

> *I have to be willing to risk negative reviews, the book having mistakes and people not liking it. Yes, it is worth the risk because I have wanted to write a book for three decades and when I look at the fears there is nothing worthy of blocking forward movement.*

What if we just decided that if you truly have the desire to create / make / become something then you can absolutely do it? What would you think and feel then?

Then I am wasting time by hesitating and doubting myself. Just get on with it. It makes me feel still inside.

If I now know I am good enough to write and publish this book then I will just break down the tasks and do the writing and publishing tasks.

If I now know that I am the right person to write this book, then I will prioritise finishing it.

If I now know that other people actually really want me to publish this book then I will do my best and also work to get it out fast, because if people really want this book, then I want to bring it into the world.

What will you choose to believe about yourself and what do you want to move forward on?

I am a good writer. I am the right person to write this book. This book will add value to a lot of people. I can do this. Whatever I don't know about publishing a book, I can learn or get someone to help me with. I can do this.

What action will you now take?

I will keep blocking time in my calendar to get this book published.

It only takes a single
conscious breath to
start grounding back
into your female
inner power

■ ■ ■

06

When you are feeling self-critical and want to shift out of it

Is your inner critic very loud and taking up too much space in your mind? Then keep reading.

Your inner critic is not actually trying to give you a hard time, even though that is usually the result when it is active.

Your inner critic is trying to do something good for you, often tied to keeping you safe in some kind of way. That said, when the inner critic is loud it is almost impossible to show up as your best self. When the inner critic raises its voice there is less space for joy, less space for connection and it becomes much harder to hear your intuition, as the intuitive voice often speaks in more quiet whispers.

Use this Journaling Guide when you are ready to shift out of self-critic mode and into a more self-loving and productive state. If you can approach this Journaling Guide not as a way of getting rid of your inner critic, but as a way to reframe and shift the things your critic is pointing out, you will then really feel your power. Listen to your critic with love and curiosity and you will find lots of gifts.

Let's journal.

What have you been criticising yourself for recently?

What is this criticism really about?

What is your inner critic trying to do for you or keep you away from? And why?

What is it you are longing for?

How can you either soften and have more self-compassion or change something so you can show up differently and more to your own preference?

What new beliefs will you choose?

And are there any actions to choose?

Example:

What have you been criticising yourself for recently?

Not building a new business quickly enough.

What is this criticism really about?

Fear of failure. I have taken a risk by choosing to work independently and I am fearful I won't succeed in creating enough work to feel professionally fulfilled and achieve the income I would like.

What is your inner critic trying to do for you or keep you away from? And why?

Keeping me safe from judgements. Not having my family and friends see me fail. Not having my previous colleagues see me be too self-promoting.

What is it you are longing for?

The sense of fulfilment that comes with a diary full of meaningful work. The sense of achievement that will come with a successful career transition.

How can you either soften and have more self-compassion or change something so you can show up differently and more to your own preference?

I could have more self-compassion by recognising and celebrating what I have achieved so far, and by defining milestones to measure and celebrate progress.

I could have more self-compassion by making time to meet with peers who are working through the same transition, to share experiences and recognise I am not alone.

What new beliefs will you choose?

I am doing meaningful work with clients.

I have the capability and drive to create my new business.

I am doing the right things to grow my business.

And are there any actions to choose?

To celebrate the milestones involved in building the business.

To gather formal feedback from clients to build a library of testimonials for future reference.

To arrange to meet with a friend who is going through a similar career transition.

Love yourself extra while you are shifting and the transformation will come faster

■ ■ ■

07

When you want to dial up your self-love

Loving yourself is one of the keys to a happy, fulfilled life. We tend to be happy to love the parts of ourselves that we are proud of. But there are parts of us we dislike and often that is where our self-love drops. But how real is the love if you are only willing to love certain aspects of yourself?

This Journaling Guide will help you dial up unconditional self-love. It will encourage you to love everything that is you. You also get to write honestly about the parts that you have struggled to love.

Growing up most of us don't get taught to speak lovingly to ourselves so you might find it slightly awkward at first. But suspend any self-judgement and just write. The rewards of doing this exercise are far greater than any self-consciousness you might experience.

You are writing to yourself in the third person to capture an honest and connecting declaration of love. Once you are done writing, I would love for you to read your love declaration out loud to yourself. Save it and read it again on another day as often as it feels good or until you feel that it has integrated.

Use the sentence prompts below that speak to you. Adapt and skip them as it feels good.

Allow yourself to be surprised and to let in the love.

Let's journal.

What I really love about you is… and… and… and…

Because …

In the past / Some days I have struggled to love these parts of you …

But I now see that you are human and I now commit to loving all parts of you.

I have held back on loving you unconditionally because I was afraid that … and because I believed …

But you deserve to feel fully loved.

Because I love you unconditionally, going forward I will remember to tell you … and arrange … for you … and say no to … for you …

If there was a mother of the universe who loved all her beings unconditionally here is what I imagine she would want you to know, hear, feel, see ….

And finally….

Example:

> *What I really love about you is how much you care about your family and how well you take care of your team members. You are truly in your integrity and I love that you always take responsibility for your part and you are open to learn.*
>
> *Because you are doing your best to live your values and I really appreciate that you want to keep being a better leader and a better human.*
>
> *In the past few months I have struggled to love the part of you that was snappy with your partner and that was negative in meetings. I don't like it when you are snappy and negative.*
>
> *But I now see that you are human and I now commit to loving all parts of you.*
>
> *I have held back on loving you unconditionally because I was afraid that if I loved the snappy and negative parts of you, you might stay like that and think that it is OK to show up like that. And I believed that if I was harsh on you, then you would do better.*
>
> *But you deserve to feel fully loved.*
>
> *Because I love you unconditionally going forward I will remember to tell you that you are amazing. That it is OK for you to have bad days. I will arrange time-outs for you where you don't have to be anything for anybody and I will arrange more Pilates classes. And I will say no to more things when your intuition is clear that it doesn't serve you.*

If there was a mother of the universe who loved all her beings unconditionally here is what I imagine she would want you to know, hear, feel, see: That you are a precious human and that you are doing well. That the kinder you are to yourself the better you will thrive. That being kind to yourself doesn't mean not growing or raising your standards. I believe in you. You get to feel loved and special right now – because you are.

And finally, I want you to know that you are always, no matter what, worthy of love.

Your inner child
wants to know that
you love all parts of
her. Only then can
she stop needing to
prove herself and
fully flourish

■ ■ ■

08

When you want to feel solid about your own value

Sometimes we need to remind ourselves of how accomplished and amazing we are, so we can show up solid and confident. This is particularly helpful if you are looking to attract or win a new opportunity or you have landed an opportunity but feel some lack of confidence.

I have seen time and again what the difference is between those who get a promotion, a new prestigious job or win the big client contract and those who don't – even though they are equally qualified and talented. The difference is very much about the certainty they have about their value. It is not arrogance. It is a grounded inner knowledge that others can feel.

What sets you apart is your genuine belief in yourself. A belief that you are a match for a great opportunity whether others see it or not. You don't need a job interview or a conversation to validate you. And you show up without any neediness because you know that if you don't get this particular opportunity, you will get something even better.

You can cultivate that kind of helpful self-belief with this Journaling Guide.

I call this exercise the 100 reasons why.

Make a list of:

100 reasons why you are the right person for this job.

100 reasons why you are a great people leader.

100 reasons why people will want to buy your products / services.

100 reasons why your company / clients will be happy to pay you double.

You might think I could never get to 100.

Well, what if you could?

Set your timer for 15 minutes and aim to get as close to 100 as you can. Then you can save this list. Read it later and add to it another day. Writing it, reading it and adding to it will help you believe in yourself.

You might think I can only come up with 5-10 reasons why. But if I had asked you to write a self-criticism list I am sure you could reach 100 reasons quickly.

Consider what you would criticise yourself and others for. And if they are things you hardly ever do, then add the positive version of that on your 100 reasons why list.

For example: If you would criticise yourself for mostly being late to meetings but you almost always are on time, you can add this as one point on your list of 100. You could write: You can count on me showing up and on time.

Add each of your experiences, each of your qualifications, each of your character traits and specific situations you have handled onto the list. Each one gets added as a separate item on the list. So, if you have 10 qualifications that is number 1-10 done on your list. If you have 20 character traits that make you attractive for this opportunity, then they each get a separate line. They all help make you the right person for the thing you want to believe you are the right person for.

It is really important to remember that all the tough things you have navigated though in life will make you a stronger candidate (assuming that you learned and grew from them), so add those items even if they are not directly related to the opportunity.

For example:

> *Going through a divorce and learning to co-parent in a conscious way has made me a better listener / leader / team member.*
>
> *Getting a concussion after a car accident taught me how to look after my body and mind and I am much more deliberate about what I need to be present in a meeting.*
>
> *Hiring someone who was the wrong fit has led me to ask different and deeper questions interviews.*

Here is a fuller example:

100 reasons why I am going to be an outstanding board member:

1. *I am going to be an outstanding board member because I am really good at listening between the lines.*

2. *I am going to be an outstanding board member because I am great at connecting the dots and seeing the bigger picture.*

3. *I am going to be an outstanding board member because I am great at speaking the truth in a way that people can hear it.*

4. *I am going to be an outstanding board member because I have worked in international development for 15 years.*

5. *I am going to be an outstanding board member because I have worked in NGOs, in government and in private sector.*

6. *I am going to be an outstanding board member because I have studied accounting.*

7. *I am going to be an outstanding board member because I did a coaching skills course for managers that made me really good at asking powerful questions.*

8. *I am going to be an outstanding board member because I care deeply about the cause of the organisation.*

9. *I am going to be an outstanding board member because I am not afraid to say when I got something wrong.*

10. *I am going to be an outstanding board member because when I was a teenager I worked part-time as a fundraiser and had to do lots of cold calling.*

11. *I am going to be an outstanding board member because I am always willing to learn.*

12. *I am going to be an outstanding board member because I bring a proactive mindset.*

13. *I am going to be an outstanding board member because I have had to fire people in the past, so I know how to make tough decisions and also do it in a dignified way.*

    Etc..

Over to you.

Let's Journal.

Choose the name of your list: A 100 Reasons why….

Then just write.

At the end of your journaling time, look over your list. How do you feel now? Celebrate no matter how many reasons you came up with today.

Keep adding and reviewing frequently, letting yourself take in all that you are, all that you have experienced and all the value that you bring.

Your certainty in
the value you can
add changes what
becomes possible

. . .

09

When you are ready to feel more joy

Joy is such a powerful energy state. When we are feeling joy, we are positively infectious. Genuine joy is attractive and impactful.

I have also found that joy also leads to us being more productive. When we are feeling joy we act faster, focus on what matters and show up more confidently.

This Journaling Guide will have you turn towards joy and make you conscious about how and where you can add more joy to your life.

Let's journal.

What gives you joy?

What does that tell you?

What are you not enjoying and how could you perhaps enjoy that more right now?

How can you add more joy to your life overall?

What would you like to celebrate and dial up your gratitude for?

What does that tell you?

Example:

What gives you joy?

My daughter's hearty belly laugh. When I finish a project. When I see one of my team members grow. When I notice I am getting stronger and all the workout sessions are paying off.

What does that tell you?

I love seeing people I care about happy and grow. I also love the feeling of progress.

What are you not enjoying and how could you perhaps enjoy that more right now?

I am not enjoying the intense targets at work and the back-to-back meetings. And I am not enjoying cooking and cleaning. I could turn on the music when I cook and clean. That would help me enjoy it more. As for work, I am less clear on how I can add more joy. Maybe I can show up with a better attitude to the meetings.

How can you add more joy to your life overall?

Maybe I can make more time for silliness with my daughter. And invest more energy in coaching my team. I wonder if there are other things I can enjoy more. Not sure how to enjoy the work pressure but maybe I can feel prouder of what we are making happen.

What would you like to celebrate and dial up your gratitude for?

I would like to celebrate my team and all their efforts. I don't think I celebrate myself much. I would like to celebrate my 2 years in this role; maybe just by having a special dinner with my family. I am very grateful for the many choices I have in my life.

What does that tell you?

I can definitely celebrate more day to day. And it feels fun thinking about adding more joy into my life.

Joy makes you more productive

relationships & situations

Journaling Guides 10 - 14

10

When you don't know where you stand with someone

This Journaling Guide is great to shift your energy around a relationship that feels full of question marks in an unhelpful way. Perhaps it is a friendship that is going through a rocky patch, a boyfriend that is being vague or a work relationship that feels messy and full of uncertainty right now.

When we don't know where we stand with a person we easily end up in some kind of waiting position. It can feel very passive and we can forget we actually have the power to influence what happens next.

Even if you feel that what is going on is 98% due to the other person, whenever there is a relationship dynamic, you play a part in it.

With these journaling questions we will look at how you might be contributing to the messiness or uncertainties of the relationship. This could be about what you are holding back, what you are not sharing, how you are now only seeing the annoying parts of the person and so on.

Sometimes, we are afraid that if we speak our truth we will start an argument or even end the relationship. But not speaking up or taking action is also a choice. Use this Journaling Guide to come back into your power and choose what you want to feel and do - regardless of what the other person does next.

In tricky situations where we are emotionally invested, it can also help to adopt a more 'neutral' perspective, as if you are witnessing the relationship dynamic from a slight distance. This usually makes it easier to understand what might be going on for the other person and can make choosing your next step faster.

Let's journal.

Why do you not know where you stand with this person?

What impact is the uncertainty in this relationship having on you?

What judgements are you holding towards this person?

While you are judging the person, what impact is it having on you? And how are you reacting?

What part are you playing in keeping this relationship in limbo? In your uncertainty about where you stand with the person, what are you doing or not doing?

No matter what happens next with this person, what are you are grateful for in terms of previous interactions, gifts or lessons from that relationship?

What do you want to feel about yourself no matter what happens with this person? And what do you want to believe?

What do you think is going on for the other person in general? And in relation to you?

From a more neutral place where you have compassion for yourself and the other person, what would you like to say or do?

Scan what you have written. What stands out for you? What is important for you to remember and do?

Example:

Why do you not know where you stand with this person?

Because we used to see each other many times a week and speak all the time and now she is hardly available.

What impact is the uncertainty in this relationship having on you?

It is making me very sad and lonely. I have definitely felt hurt. And frustrated.

What judgements are you holding towards this person?

That she is not there for me. That she is totally wrapped up in her own world. She doesn't have capacity for much.

While you are judging the person, what impact is it having on you? And how are you reacting?

It is bringing out a very negative judgemental part of me. And I am flipping between wanting her to feel hurt too and just withdrawing and cutting her off completely. Neither feels good.

What part are you playing in keeping this relationship in limbo? In your uncertainty about where you stand with the person what are you doing or not doing?

I have told her some of what I am feeling and then it got better for a while. But now it is weird again and I haven't been fully honest about how much it hurts me. So I guess my part is pretending that I am OK with how things are right now.

No matter what happens next with this person, what are you are grateful for in terms of previous interactions, gifts or lessons from that relationship?

I am grateful for the many fun times we have had together, here and abroad, and for all the cups of tea and chats. Many fun precious memories and experiences. Also, she was there for me through some tricky times. Her support was absolutely priceless.

What do you want to feel about yourself no matter what happens with this person? And what do you want to believe?

I want to feel happy and supported. I want to believe that this relationship will work out for the highest good for both of us. And that there are wonderful humans that could fill the gap of this friendship if she continues to be unavailable.

What do you think is going on for the other person in general? And in relation to you?

I think she is in a major transition of life. Her schedule got very busy recently and she is struggling to fit in things she had time for previously. I don't think it has much to do about me. I think she cares deeply for me but doesn't have much to give right now.

From a more neutral place where you have compassion for yourself and the other person, what would you like to say or do?

I am not sure whether I want to tell her that I will withdraw more. But maybe. I kind of want to acknowledge that our relationship is different right now and that it has shifted a lot. But I would like to do this without judgement. Though I do want to share that I miss her.

Scan what you have written. What stands out for you? What is important for you to remember and do?

When I looked at what's going on for her it is easier to feel compassion and get out of judgement. I don't want to pretend. So I do want to speak some truth in a way that is compassionate towards both of us.

It is in your power to feel what you want to feel no matter what

■ ■ ■

11

When you are finding a people dynamic frustrating

This is for when you are finding yourself in a tricky work dynamic or when a personal relationship is feeling challenging. We can spend ages stuck in frustration with another human being and that can be a major energy leak.

People dynamics tend to be frustrating because one or several of our needs are not being met or because something clashes with our values. When we show up needy we will never be as graceful as we would like to be. And when our values are confronted, we tend to feel furious.

We can never change or control others, but we can take responsibility to meet our own needs and explore how we can show up more in our power. When we do that, we will have much more resilience to deal with and patience to be with other humans. This is taking responsibility for our part of the dynamic.

Let's journal.

What is it about the dynamic that is challenging?

Why does it bother you?

What are you doing / not doing in relation to the other person or people in this dynamic? And why?

What do you see the other person do or not do? How are they acting in relation to you?

Let's decide for a moment that the other person's behaviour in relation to you isn't personal. In fact, if there was another person in your shoes the dynamic would be the same. From that perspective what is this really about?

What is it that you need and want? And are there any of your personal values that are in a clash or not being met?

How could you get your needs met? And if not in this situation with this person where else or how else could they be met?

Is there anything else you can do or say to make sure your values are respected and met?

Going forward what would you like to think, believe and do differently to break your side of the dynamic?

Scan what you have written so far. What else would be helpful?

Example:

What is it about the dynamic that is challenging?

He doesn't include me or ask me for input.

Why does it bother you?

Because I have done so much work on this client account and he hasn't. He might be more senior, but I have been on the ground in the client doing the work and building the relationships. If I hadn't done a great job we would not be getting business from that client five years later.

What are you doing / not doing in relation to the other person or people in this dynamic? And why?

I am just getting on with the assignment, but I am not communicating with the Managing Partner. Since I don't receive recognition and I don't get invited in on new proposals, even though I have said several times I want to be involved, then I can't be bothered any more.

What do you see the other person do or not do? How are they acting in relation to you?

He doesn't do much in relation to me. I imagine he just expects me to get on with it. And I imagine this is not his main priority. Actually, more than that, I think he might just be a bit tired of it all. A bit jaded.

Let's decide for a moment that the other person's behaviour in relation to you isn't personal. In fact, if there was another person in your shoes the dynamic would be the same. From that perspective what is this really about?

He is not excited or invested in making this client grow. He is busy and assumes that I will be more proactive than I have been. He is also not aware that I feel unacknowledged or rejected. Probably because he doesn't get a lot of appreciation himself, so he doesn't see anything missing here.

What is it that you need and want? And are there any of your personal values that are in a clash or not being met?

I need appreciation. And I would like to do more projects with this client. In terms of values it is a about connection and partnership for me. I don't feel that the Managing Partner is interested in much connection or partnership with me.

How could you get your needs met? And if not in this situation with this person where else or how else could they be met?

In terms of appreciation I do get it from the client and I can also give that to myself. And in terms of more work from this client, I can speak to the Managing Partner about my ideas again. I can also pitch some of my ideas directly to the client.

Is there anything else you can do or say to make sure your values are respected and met?

I actually think the Managing Partner values partnership and connection, just like me. I just think he is tired. He is close to retirement age. I think I would need to take the initiative if I wanted anything to change.

Going forward what would you like to think, believe and do differently to break your side of the dynamic?

I definitely don't want to be annoyed with the Managing Partner anymore because that is a waste of energy. I want to enjoy the client work, appreciate myself and be proactive. I will consider speaking to the Managing Partner about connection and partnership but not from a place of criticising him, rather from a place of "we have had a bit of this some years ago and I would like more of it".

Scan what you have written so far. What else would be helpful?

Remembering my power. Choosing to focus on all the good things in the situations. And creating my own luck.

May it work out for
the highest good for
all involved

■ ■ ■

12

When you want to feel appreciated

When we want to feel appreciated or when feel that we are (over)due some appreciation, we can easily become resentful and deflated. Clearly that doesn't serve us.

The thing is, as much as you might rightfully deserve appreciation, being needy about it won't bring you any good.

In some ways the need for appreciation is about feeling validated. Tell me I am a good leader / mother / colleague / project lead etc. Validate me. And thank me.

While we are looking for validation there is no way we can be our best selves. We become needy. And resentful.

The people who we think should give us this acknowledgment and thanks might be distracted, forgetful, not great at noticing how much we have actually done and very likely stuck in their own stuff. You could wait for them to notice your efforts and you could wait for them to give you the appreciative feedback. But it may or may not come. And while you are waiting, you will feel passive. The waiting also puts your own ability to be appreciated in the hands of other people, so the power is in their hands, not yours.

For this Journaling Guide to have the impact of making you feel better, it is important that we let go of the demand that the appreciation must come from a specific human or group of humans. If they give it to you, that is great, but what if we never needed to wait anyway to receive appreciation and validation from an outside source?

For now, let's decide that no matter whether the other humans can find the words and gestures that would show you appreciation, you get to feel appreciated right now. You get to have fun appreciating yourself on their behalf. This Guide can be used for work and non-work situations equally well.

Let's journal.

Who would you like to appreciate you and your efforts more? And why?

What are you wishing they would appreciate, acknowledge and properly thank you for?

Now write the most genuine, delicious and detailed appreciation-letter to yourself in the third person. Make sure to include the things you are longing to be appreciated and acknowledged for. You can decide this letter is from the Universe, from yourself or from someone else. Make it feel good.

Use these prompts as inspiration.

Dear [your name]

I am so thankful that you helped make … happen.

Without you … wouldn't have been possible / been this amazing and without your contribution …

I see how much you …

And I want to acknowledge that you are a true …

Please allow my appreciation to fill up your heart and soul.

Your work is deeply appreciated.

If you want to make this extra powerful you can read this letter out loud to yourself. Read it to yourself in the third person.

Example:

Who would you like to appreciate you and your efforts more? And why?

> *I wish my boss would truly appreciate how much work I have put in over the last six months. This merger has taken insane energy and hours. I have been close to burnout.*

What are you wishing they would appreciate, acknowledge and properly thank you for?

> *I wish he would thank me for working all these extra hours and I know there is more coming because there is still more merger work. I would like him to notice that I never complain but I just handle things and get on with it. I would like him to appreciate*

how I take care of my team and their needs, despite the pressure on me, they are still thriving. I have sacrificed a lot in terms of my family and my evenings and this wasn't the deal when I took the job.

....

Dear Lydia

I am so thankful that you worked all these extra hours during the merger.

Without you this merger would have been a lot messier because we were able to rely on you to take action, ask important questions, help the teams on both sides connect the dots and you always do it happily.

I see how much you give of yourself and your time and your positive energy uplifts us all.

And I want to acknowledge that you are a true team player and leader. It is rare that people can do great pro-active leadership and non-ego team playing at the same time. Thank you for who you are, and for how you rise to every challenge. When you took the job, the brief was very different, but you grew fast. Your team is always thriving and getting on with things and I know so much of that has to do with you.

Please accept my genuine appreciation and respect.

I could not do my job without you. Thank you. I really mean that. Truly thank you. And yes I do hope I can get you another pay rise or bonus soon.

With gratitude from the Universe (and your boss and all the people involved in the merger)

When you genuinely appreciate yourself without needing appreciation from others, you will show up more grounded

■ ■ ■

13

When you want to be in your power regarding a challenging situation

How can you be more at your best when you find yourself in a situation that is challenging for you?

When we are frustrated with a situation, we easily end up spending most of our energy on everything that is wrong. We might end up focused on things that are out of our hands.

Although it might be true that some things in a situation are out of our control, we always have the power to choose what thoughts we want to cultivate and what feelings we want to reach for. This doesn't mean it is easy to do this, so love yourself extra as you work on shifting your energy in a tricky situation, because it will take some effort.

To shift you into your power in a difficult situation we will play with this concept: What if there is a hidden gift in this situation? What if the fact that you are in this situation is actually "perfect" in some weird way?

It could be perfect because there is something for you to learn here. Perhaps it is a chance to get clarity on something, maybe there is something to let go of or perhaps this means it is time to turn your attention and focus in a different direction.

We all know that we learn the most from the challenges in our life, so what might be the "gift" from this situation?

Let's journal.

Allow yourself first to release your frustration. What feels frustrating and difficult about this situation?

What is this frustration really about and what are you actually afraid of?

Then take a moment to breathe.

Notice how you have unconsciously given that situation (or person involved in the situation) the power. You are not feeling what you want to feel because of something outside of yourself. Which means you have given away your power. This hurts each time I realise this for myself. Ouch.

Let's shift you into your power again. What if the fact that you are in this situation is actually perfect? This might be the perfect situation because it is helping you …

What are the potential hidden gifts of this situation that you might only be able to see later on? How can you grow from this situation?

What is in your power with regards to this situation?

What do you want to do, to make the most of this situation while you are in it?

How can you already feel better about this situation right now?

What else is important for you to remember in relation to this situation?

Any other choices or insights?

Take a breath to thank yourself for doing this work. You are doing well. You are taking responsibility for shifting your state of thinking and that is making the world better. Thank you for doing your work.

Example:

Allow yourself first to release your frustration. What feels frustrating and difficult about this situation?

> *So many changes at work that I didn't wish for. I feel it is stupid that these changes are being made. And I feel bad for my team. I see a big risk that everything we have worked for might be lost. We will have a difficult time ahead due to organisational changes. What is hopeful is that the Execs seem to listen to my ideas somewhat. I do have some influence.*

What is this frustration really about and what are you actually afraid of?

> *I am most afraid to lose the connection with our customers. I am afraid of not being able to deliver good work, because I have to spread myself too thin over so many different projects.*

Let's shift you into your power again. What if the fact that you are in this situation is actually perfect? This might be the perfect situation because it is helping you …

The change can give me the opportunity to deep dive into our core methodology and research. To build a connection with people who complement my strengths. Or even better to be able to practice and to inspire others to become more innovative within constraints.

What are the potential hidden gifts of this situation that you might only be able to see later on? How can you grow from this situation?

Because of all this change I can't just continue to do what I have done so far. I know, I will grow a lot from this situation. I will probably become better at business management and innovation because that is now required. And I can meet new people and expand my network.

What is in your power with regards to this situation?

How I want to pass on the messages to my team. What energy and attitude I show up with. How proactive I get with maximising the learning opportunities here.

What do you want to do, to make the most of this situation while you are in it?

I want to help my team reflect on what opportunities this reorganisation and all the changes can bring for them. I want to help them grow and become better leaders in this period of change.

How can you already feel better about this situation right now?

It feels good thinking about how I can make it better for my team. And I like the idea of them looking back on this period of their career saying that this helped them become more resilient and more innovative.

What else is important for you to remember in relation to this situation?

In some ways this could be one of the most rewarding team experiences. If we pull together around what is possible, then we can all grow so much and feel better by being in it together.

Any other choices or insights?

I want to remember I am valuable. And I want to focus on making sure I and my team reflect and learn every day.

The past does not equal the future

■ ■ ■

14

When you are in a situation or period with a lot of uncertainty and unknown

Life is often full of unknowns. Sometimes that is exciting. At other times it can feel overwhelming. With uncertainty around bigger things in life, we can turn to predicting what could go wrong and as a consequence activate our internal fear. We can also end up not taking much action as we wait for more information.

This self-coaching Journaling Guide will help you be more at your best in that kind of situation. We want to focus on pro-actively choosing what you want to feel and looking at what moves you can make no matter what.

Let's focus on your power and create "a story" you want to live. At some point this period will be over. What you decide to think, feel and do right now, will likely have significant impact on what becomes possible.

Let's journal.

What is going on and what is unknown or uncertain?

What is known / certain? And what are you grateful for?

What are you fearful of?

Is what you are afraid of likely to happen? If yes could you handle it even if you wouldn't enjoy it?

How are the fears and worries about the unknown impacting you?

What can you do right now to impact the unknown positively and minimise the risks you fear?

All great heroes go through periods of unknown. Imagine that the current period is a chapter in the book of your life. Imagine that this chapter is one of those that makes the reader really impressed with how you pick yourself up and lead yourself.

Write down what you will be telling yourself, or focusing on, or doing in order to make this chapter of your life one that you will be super proud of. You can let yourself be inspired by these prompts.

This was the chapter of my life where I….

And I am so proud of how I …

What I focused on and what helped me was ….

What could help make this period of uncertainty more enjoyable?

What do you want to tell yourself and what do you want to feel through this period?

Scan what you have written. What is most important? And what will help you feel in your power right now?

Example:

What is going on and what is unknown or uncertain?

I lost my job. We have enough savings for a while. But I do need to find another job. I can feel my confidence starting to be a bit shaky.

What is known / certain? And what are you grateful for?

I love my family. I am grateful for where we live. We are healthy. I have a lot of experience. Many people have lost their job and come through it just fine.

What are you fearful of?

I am afraid that we will use up all our savings. Or go into debt. I am afraid that it will take me a really long time to get a new job. I am afraid that I will have to take a job I won't like. Most of all, I am afraid of disappointing my family.

Is what you are afraid of likely to happen? If yes could you handle it even if you wouldn't enjoy it?

Is it likely that my family will be disappointed in me and that it will take me a long time to find a job? I don't know. I know my family loves me. Can I handle it if it is financially tough? Well, if other people can I guess so can I.

How are the fears and worries about the unknown impacting you?

> *They are making me nervous, less confident. Feeling low.*

What can you do right now to impact the unknown positively and minimise the risks you fear?

> *I think what is most important is that I keep my energy and my mood high. Exercise definitely helps. Connecting with all kinds of people in my network but not from a needy place. Rather from a place of thinking about how I can help them. And of course, applying for jobs.*

All great heroes go through periods of unknown. Imagine that the current period is a chapter in the book of your life. Imagine that this chapter is one of those that makes the reader really impressed with how you pick yourself up and lead yourself.

Write down what you will be telling yourself, or focusing on, or doing in order to make this chapter of your life one that you will be super proud of:

> *This was the chapter of my life where I learned so much about my inner strength. I am so proud of how I chose to be focused in my days, exercise, be there for the family, and focus on what I was grateful for. It helped me to focus on helping other people. Reminding myself how valuable I am. I kept reminding myself of how I can add value in so many contexts and then I took action. And I invested in myself in several ways because I believe that I would be worth it.*

What could help make this period of uncertainty more enjoyable?

> *Enjoying the space that not having full time work gives. Making sure I do some of the things I always said I would if I didn't work.*

What do you want to tell yourself and what do you want to feel through this period?

> *I will come through it. I can handle a tough period. I will come out of this stronger. I want to feel grounded and calm. And I want to focus on all the good that is here.*

Scan what you have written. What is most important? And what will help you feel in your power right now?

> *I have space and freedom and I can enjoy it. Helping others will make me feel better about myself. I only need one job. Worrying won't help me. This could be an amazing period of my life.*

What if the best is yet to come?

■ ■ ■

leadership & decision-making

Journaling Guides 15 - 19

15

When you need quick clarity about your work priorities

"I have to schedule some time to get clarity and prioritise". I cannot tell you how many times I have heard clients tell me that over the years. Or: "I will block two hours on Friday to prioritise." Countless variations of those two phrases.

I usually reply by saying: "No you don't" My confused client will look through the Zoom window and wonder if I really meant No. Did my coach really say don't schedule time to prioritise, they wonder.

Yes - your coach meant it when she said no. Because there is no point in scheduling time. You already know what matters. No reason to complicate things. The simple and clear answers are available right in this minute.

Let's backtrack quickly.

If you are like most of the amazing humans I have the privilege of coaching, you have way more tasks than you have time for. You have lists of lists and meetings following meetings. No time to pause, no time to think.

This results in overwhelm and lack of clarity. Often accompanied with low-grade anxiety from feeling like you are not getting enough done and a sense that you are not getting to that which is most important, because it isn't urgent.

If this is even vaguely familiar, this Journaling Guide is for you.

It works every time. I have tested it so many times. Write down the first answers that come to you. Don't overthink this. Trust yourself.

Then make sure to act in alignment with that clarity.

Let's journal.

Imagine that your inbox has crashed and that no email can be recovered. Your calendar is totally wiped and all to-do lists and project plans have vanished too. Now close your eyes, breathe for a moment and then ask yourself: What are the 3 most important priorities in my work right now?

For each of the three priorities, why does this priority really matter and what is this really about?

And if you want to get even more practical: How can you make time to work on those priorities today and the rest of this week?

What will you delete, delegate, reschedule or say no to, to make space for these 3 most important priorities?

Example:

I am not going to give you a full example here, but I want to reassure you that this works even if someone is completely new in a job. Then, usually, the answers go something like this.

> *Top 3 priorities: 1. Listen deeply and connect with as many people in the organisation as possible. 2. Listen for where both my role and I can add value 3. Understand how communication and systems work in this organisation.*

Notice how the answers are not a specific task. The answers are more like filters. So, when you get invited to a meeting or write a to-do list, you can check in with your 3 answers and see if this meeting/task will help you with your 3 key priorities. If not, then maybe it is not supposed to take your focus and time.

Try also using this journaling exercise for your non-work life.

You always know
what matters

■ ■ ■

16

When you want to be confident about a work decision and know whether fear or courage is in charge

Are you hesitating about making a work decision? Perhaps you are doubting which decision to make and how to decide?

This Journaling Guide will strengthen your confidence in your decision making. You will understand more about what sways your decisions and have a greater appreciation for what underlying forces influence your ability to decide.

The 7 decision prompts below are set up for a work / business / leadership decision but you can modify them to use for a non-work decision as well.

Give yourself the gift of 10 minutes to answer these quickly and intuitively. Don't censor anything. Just be curious.

Let's journal.

The 7 decision prompts:

What do you need to make a decision about?

Next finish these sentences intuitively:

1. **If I let fear take the lead in this situation – the decision will be …**

2. **If I do what is expected by my boss / investor / stakeholder – the decision will be …**

3. **If I do as I was taught growing up – the decision will be …** (Don't skip this one about the childhood learnings, as tempting as it might be. The insights here might highlight deeper, perhaps even unconscious patterns. See the example for more details if you are stuck)

4. **If I do what my customers / clients prefer, the decision will be …**

5. **If I make the same decision I think my most successful competitors / peers would make, the decision will be…**

6. **If I make a choice which is overall best for everyone involved, the decision will be …**

7. **If I am filled with unconditional courage and faith, the decision will be …**

Which answers surprised you?

What decision do you want to make? (Perhaps you will take elements from several of the answers)

What did you learn about yourself and decision making?

Example:

For this Journaling Guide I just want to give you an expansion around decision prompt 3: "If I do as I was taught growing up, the decision will be …" Sometimes clients go blank on this prompt and if you find that you don't get an immediate answer, ask yourself: What would my mother think is the right decision in this kind of situation and why? Or: What would my dad think is the right thing to do here and why?

A client of mine used the mother / father prompts when deciding what to do about a long-term underperforming team member. She journaled that her mother would have wanted to give the team member another chance, because she only wanted to see the best in everyone. Her dad would have said it was overdue to tell this team member to pull their weight, because the rest of the team was working extra to compensate. These insights were massively helpful for my client to understand some of her internal tensions and she chose to use the best of both. The straight-talking from her dad delivered with the compassion of her mother.

You can handle
getting it wrong

Make a decision and
act on it

■ ■ ■

17

When you want to improve your leadership

This is for when you want to reflect on your leadership. Whether you are in an organisational leadership role or running your own business, this Journaling Guide will be helpful. Even if you are not in an official leadership role, consider going through the questions anyway and just adapting them to fit your context.

Great leaders are always looking to learn, grow and improve.

Let's journal.

What are you proud of when it comes to your leadership and work in the last 1-3 months?

What are you learning about yourself as a leader / business owner?

What do you wish you would be better at? And what do you think is blocking you from shifting or improving this?

How can you start improving this right now?

If you showed up as your very best self with endless energy, what would you do differently or handle better? And what does that tell you?

Looking at what you have journaled, what can you now do and put in place to make sure your leadership is improving? What accountability will you set up and what new experiments?

Example:

What are you proud of when it comes to your leadership and work in the last 1-3 months?

> *I have really been there for my team.*

What are you learning about yourself as a leader?

> *I am still looking to prove myself and I find it hard when I don't get any feedback. I can get impatient and very directive when there is pressure to meet a deadline.*

What do you wish you would be better at? And what do you think is blocking you from shifting or improving this?

> *I would like to be calmer under pressure. I would like to stop feeling like I have to prove myself.*

What are the blocks to these?

> *Actually, they are linked. Ha, just saw it. Because I fear I am not good enough and think I have to prove myself, I get really stressed when there is an important deadline.*

How can you start improving this right now?

Believing that I am good enough. Each time I want to prove myself I become stressed in a bad way. Might need to get some help to really believe in myself. Don't know why that is still so hard for me.

If you showed up as your very best self with endless energy, what would you do differently or handle better? And what does that tell you?

I would dare to be more visionary and bolder on next year's strategy. I would play to win rather than play to make sure I don't get it wrong. This tells me I am still led by fear.

Looking at what you have journaled, what can you now do and put in place to make sure your leadership is improving? What accountability will you set up and what new experiments?

I can invite a cross-section of colleagues to explore next year's strategy to challenge and stretch my thinking. I will look for some 1:1 coaching to work on my need to prove myself. And I want to speak to my mentor about all of it.

Extraordinary leaders
are great students

■ ■ ■

18

When you want to evaluate how you are spending your time

The most precious resource we have is time. I am sure you have heard the saying that we cannot manage time. All we can do is manage ourselves.

So, if you care about a life well-lived, showing up as your best self, making an impact, really making something of what life offers (or however you want to phrase it), looking at how you use your time, is massively important. Once today is gone, it is gone.

Note: Spending time isn't just about how many minutes you are actively pursuing or working on something. It is also the amount of time you spend leaking energy to something. For example, when we are nervous about a conversation, we spend much more time and energy worrying about how the conversation might play out than the actual time it takes for us to speak with the person.

Someone wise once said: Show me your schedule and I will tell you what your priorities are. This Journaling Guide will help you take an honest look at where your time and energy go.

You can journal on how you spend time overall in your life or you can narrow in on one part of your life. I suggest trying both and seeing what you learn.

Let's journal.

How are you spending your time at the moment? And how does that add value to you, your life and / or your work?

What are you spending time on that gives you energy?

What are you spending time on that drains your energy?

What would you like to stop spending time / energy on?

If you trust that you have the power to change your life, how can you stop spending time / energy on that now? Or at least move towards that, by gradually spending less and less time on it?

Who and what would benefit from having you be more present and conscious?

What would you like to make time for?

If you want to be more impactful and be at your best more of the time, what do you need to spend more time on?

What does this make you realise?

What are your choices and action steps?

Example:

How are you spending your time at the moment? And how does that add value to you, your life and / or your work?

> *I am working on setting up my new business. I am also spending time with my son. But I find it hard to get the business off the ground and be a mum.*

What are you spending time on that gives you energy?

> *Planning the new business. Saturday playground fun. The three of us cooking nice Sunday brunches.*

What are you spending time on that drains your energy?

> *I think it is mostly the way I worry and stress that takes my energy. Also, admin and house work.*

What would you like to stop spending time / energy on?

> *Admin and house work. And I would like to stop worrying.*

If you trust that you have the power to change your life, how can you stop spending time / energy on that now? Or at least move towards that, by gradually spending less and less time on it?

> *I am not ready to spend money on a cleaner, but I can definitely worry less. What will help me is to trust myself more. And also, to trust that even if the business isn't successful I am learning and it will still*

be worth it. That something good will come from this no matter what.

Who and what would benefit from having you be more present and conscious?

My son. My husband. And if I worry less and trust more, my work will benefit too.

What would you like to make time for?

More walks in nature. Reading good quality fiction.

If you want to be more impactful and be at your best more of the time, what do you need to spend more time on?

Probably networking more if it is business impact. If it is family, it is not necessarily about more time. It is just about me being able to enjoy family time more.

What does this make you realise?

Going for walks is an easy thing to make time for. I can also make sure to set up virtual coffees every week to strengthen my connections and network. Some changes are very easy to make.

What are your choices and action steps?

I want to enjoy this period and tell myself that no matter what working on building a business will be worthwhile.

Do something today
that your future self
will thank you for

■ ■ ■

19

When you want to set your intentions for the month ahead

At the end of 2020, when I started seeing all the emails about setting goals for the next year, I felt totally uninspired. The COVID pandemic had hit the world that year; so many plans had been cancelled, so many goals no longer made sense.

Still, I wanted to create some kind of planning and intention-setting session for the year ahead. That is when the Female Inner Power approach to planning was born. I tested it for myself. Then I shared it during several group workshops to rave reviews.

My clients loved looking at how they wanted to feel and what they wanted to think for the year ahead. They loved that the intention-setting was about starting from the inside out.

Below you will find a Journaling Guide designed to help you set intentions for the month ahead, based on the Female Inner Power planning approach.

Let's journal

1. **Things you already know that will take place or have a deadline this month:**

2. **Things you would like to do / experience or complete this month:**

3. **How would you like to feel this month?**

4. **What thoughts would you like to think frequently this month?**

5. **What do you want to let go of this month? (Might be a habit, obligation or a thought)**

6. **What is something you are apprehensive or nervous about this month? How would you like to show up for it?**

7. **What would you like to be proud of at the end of this month? And what would make you super happy this month?**

8. **What actions can you take within the next few days to move towards those things that will make you proud and happy?**

9. **What self-nourishment and support are you lining up so you can spend more time at your best?**

10. **What mantra or belief do you want to choose to strengthen you for the month?**

11. **Scan what you have written. What stands out for you? What does this tell you?**

Example:

Instead of giving you a full example, I want to go deeper on question 4. What thoughts would you like to think frequently this month?

I really love giving time to this question and in a way planning my month through answering it. I have lots of fun writing the thoughts just as I wish to hear them in my mind during the upcoming month. This is a very powerful way of influencing how you will experience the next month and a reminder of how you can choose your thoughts and stories.

For example, you might imagine that when difficult things happen for the next month you will choose to think: I have got this. I can do this. I know I can find the right helper for this situation. And you might also want to think: This project is really coming together. I love working with my client on this. Things are moving really fast in such a good way. I always have time for both work and family.

If you want to make this even more powerful I suggest writing or speaking these thoughts out every morning of that month.

Restating the thoughts we want to have might seem odd, but if you think about how easily we fall into habitual thinking loops, you will appreciate that daily repetition is required to make new thoughts stick. Give it a go and watch what happens.

Book Bonus: If you want to learn more about how to reprogram your mind with new beliefs and upgrade your thoughts, then sign up to the free short training on Installing New Beliefs.

Go to www.noominatan.com/bonus for instant access to this practical training.

Every day is a chance
to grow and develop

Ask yourself: What
have I learned today?
Write it down and let
it in

■ ■ ■

possibilities & momentum

Journaling Guides 20 - 25

20

When you are procrastinating and want to shift into momentum

This Journaling Guide is for when you want to take action and create momentum, but for whatever reason (or perhaps lots of reasons) you are stuck hesitating, procrastinating or even waiting.

Before we get journaling I want to share four things about procrastination.

- Underneath procrastination is often fear. Fear that something might go wrong. Or fear that something might go right. We are often (unconsciously) afraid of change. Status quo is what we know, so generating momentum towards our dreams and desires can make us nervous about what we might expose ourselves to or have to overcome.
- Another reason why we procrastinate is that we forget to break things down into actual next steps.

  For example, if you are procrastinating around learning to invest, you might have written 'learn to invest' on your to-do list. But 'learn to invest' is not one thing. When you are working through your task list, and that is what it says, it is very tricky to know what you are actually supposed to do. What helps create momentum is to consciously take another step in the direction of learning to invest. What doesn't help is spending lots of time wondering what the "right" next step is or spending significant amounts of time preparing yourself to take the next step.

The next step in learning to invest could be: To listen to an audiobook about investing. To ask a friend who invests if you can buy them coffee and learn from them. To sign up to a seminar about investing. To ask ChatGPT how you can start. There is no single correct next step. You choose. What works is to take the next step. It also really helps to make the next step something easy and to tell yourself that it is no big deal. Because whenever we make something a big deal, we tend to freeze. Then once you have taken the next step, take another step as soon as possible.

- If you feel accountable to someone it will be easier for you to stop hesitating and to take action. Depending on what you want momentum on, you might have automatic accountability in the form of a boss or a partner. But if not, definitely ask a great friend or colleague to support you with your wish to move forward. Tell them what you will do and by when. Then request that they lovingly call you out on your excuses if you don't keep your word.
- Finally, reminding ourselves of why something matters to us helps fuel us. Tune in often to the deeper reason why you want momentum instead of hesitation.

Let's journal.

What are you procrastinating about moving forward on?

What are you afraid that might happen if you move forward? (If you were sure that it would be delightful then you wouldn't be hesitating)

What is this fear really about?

Do you want this fear to rule your life? (Yes, that is a leading question)

What do you really want in relation to the thing you are procrastinating on? How do you want to feel and be around it?

Next, let's journal on the action steps you can take to get moving. Brainstorm for a moment. What are five potential next steps that you could take in the next few days?

Which one will you commit to and when will you take it?

Who will you ask to be your accountability partner?

Imagine you keep taking steps forward, gaining momentum towards your desired outcome. Feel the relief, excitement or whatever feeling you imagine you might feel when this is done. Visualise taking the different steps. Seeing yourself take the steps first in your mind will help you take them physically later.

Why is it important to you to create momentum around this thing?

Add the deadline for the next step to your calendar and make sure to take an action step as soon as possible afterwards.

Celebrate your new momentum. It is easy to look at how far

there still is to go, but that will deflate your energy and likely get you back into procrastinating. Instead, keep celebrating every step. Even if it turns out not to work.

Example:

What are you procrastinating about moving forward on?

Starting to invest.

What are you afraid might happen if you move forward?

I am afraid that I will lose more money than I will make. That I will be no good at it. That it will be hard and I will feel stupid for not being able to do it well. That I will get ripped off by all kinds of hidden fees.

What is this fear really about?

Risk-taking. I feel stupid for having cash sitting in a savings account earning less interest than inflation, but I feel scared about losing it and making mistakes. Maybe there is a fear that I am no good with money.

Do you want this fear to rule your life?

No. But it feels scary to change.

What do you really want in relation to the thing you are procrastinating on? How do you want to feel and be around it?

I want to feel proud and excited about investing. I want to start investing but without putting pressure on myself so just a small amount we can afford to play with. I don't want to give up before I have even tried it.

Next, let's journal on the action steps you can take to get moving. Brainstorm for a moment. What are five potential next steps that you could take in the next few days?

Read the book my friend recommended about investing.

Ask my friend who invests how she does it.

Google what I need to set up to be able to invest.

Decide how much money I will play with to start.

Those feel like the most important first steps.

Which one will you commit to and when will you take it?

Ask my friend who invests if she will show me how she does it. I will message her this evening.

Who will you ask to be your accountability partner?

I think this friend of mine would also like to hold me accountable because she has been encouraging me to get into investing.

Visualise taking the different steps.

Why is it important to you to create momentum around this thing?

There is always a risk when investing but there are also so many great opportunities. It feels strong and powerful to get better with money and explore investing.

A teeny tiny tweak
today can start a
whole new trajectory
in your life

■ ■ ■

21

When you want something to manifest or succeed faster

This Guide is for when you have wanted to make something happen for a while and it doesn't seem to be building momentum. Maybe you wanted to make a leap in your career or in your health. Maybe you wanted to shift a habitual pattern. Or perhaps you wanted to significantly increase your income. Whatever it is, either it feels like it is just not happening, or it is happening at turtle-speed and you are not sure it will ever be as big and as great as you want it to be.

Or more precisely, maybe it feels like **you** are not happening. Because you have probably seen "it" happen for others, so maybe the turtle-speed is related to you...

This Journaling Guide will help you uncover hidden blocks and beliefs, so you know what to focus on and what to shift to move towards the success you desire.

Of course, you are worthy of everything you could possibly want, but this Journaling Guide starts by asking you why you are not worthy of what you want. Let the unconscious fear-mind and inner critic come out here. Capture all the non-pretty things. This is not about revealing truth. It is about revealing where you are blocking yourself and this question will get you there fast. Afterwards, you will shift by consciously choosing new beliefs and actions.

Let's journal.

Why do you fear you are not worthy of the thing you want to create or to have on a bigger scale? (Keep writing until you feel empty)

Are there any other reasons why you don't yet have what you want? This is letting out more self-judgments.

Look at what you have written: What stands out for you? What does this tell you?

Which beliefs do you choose to change or let go of to align with what you want?

What are some more helpful beliefs that will support you to succeed?

What new actions or behaviours are you willing to commit to that can help you move faster towards what you want?

And how will you embed the new beliefs?

What do you want to take away from this session?

Example:

Why do you fear you are not worthy of the thing you want to create or to have on a bigger scale?

I want to have a big pay rise. I am ready for Director-level and I want the pay that matches. So why am I not feeling worthy? Because I am not sure I am good enough. Because there are things I don't know. Because I still want to have time to spend with my children. Because I don't want to work on the weekends. Because work is not everything to me.

Are there any other reasons why you don't yet have what you want? This is letting out more self-judgments.

I am not confident enough. I am not strategic enough. I am spending too much time in the weeds.

Look at what you have written: What stands out for you? What does this tell you?

It tells me that I want to make time for strategic work. That it is time to believe in myself and my value. And that I have some unhelpful, unconscious assumptions of what is expected of Directors.

Which beliefs do you choose to change or let go of to align with what you want?

I am ready to let go off these two beliefs: 1. Being a Director means less time with my children. 2. I am not good enough.

What are some more helpful beliefs that will support you to succeed?

I can be an amazing Director and also spend time with my children. I am already operating at Director-level. I already add tons of value.

What new actions or behaviours are you willing to commit to that can help you move faster towards what you want? And how will you embed the new beliefs?

I will ask myself daily: If I was a Director, how would I handle this? And I will remind myself that I am valuable and that it is not about how many hours I work. That in fact, being a mother makes me a better leader.

What do you want to take away from this session?

I didn't realise these old-fashioned beliefs were still under the surface. I want to look for role models, perhaps in podcast interviews of successful female leaders who also spend a lot of time with their children.

Book Bonus: If you want to learn more about how to reprogram your mind with new beliefs and upgrade your thoughts, then sign up to the free short training on Installing New Beliefs.

Go to www.noominatan.com/bonus for instant access to this practical training.

Think bigger and keep taking steps to back yourself and your dreams

■ ■ ■

22

When you want to love your life and your future more

I have had periods in my life where I woke up in the morning and declared: I love my life. I have had seasons where I told others: I love this chapter of my life. And I have also had periods where I said and thought very differently.

What we say and what we think easily become self-fulfilling prophecies. So here is a Journaling Guide focused on coaching yourself to feel gratitude and love for your life. We will mix in some manifestation techniques for what you want to be grateful for in the future too.

I cannot take credit for what is in this Guide because I have learned about gratitude from so many teachers through books, conversations, coaching and courses. To name just two, I will mention Rhonda Byrne and Bob Proctor.

When you are writing your gratitude, the aim is to get your heart and body activated so you can feel the thankfulness and appreciation. We want your energy to enter the frequency of gratitude rather than only having some grateful thoughts. But don't think too much about it. Just go with the Guide and have fun.

One of the reasons we may feel hesitant about appreciating the current moment is because of what we predict for the next moment. We predict that we will settle here; that if we are grateful for what is, then that is all that we will ever get.

This couldn't be further from the truth. The more we can be grateful for what we already have, the more goodness can come to us.

Let's journal.

1. **Write 5-10 things you are grateful for. Add why each thing is valuable to you by adding 'because' to deepen the gratitude.**

   I am grateful for … because …

2. **Then write at least 5 statements starting with the words: I love my life because... You can use the same things you wrote about in your gratitude statements or add new ones. Whatever feels good.**

   I love my life because …

Notice how these I-love-my-life statements can be about massive profound truths or small little moments. They all count equally.

3. **Let's work on manifesting a future you feel excited about. What are at least 5 things you want to happen / experience / improve in the next little while? You decide the time frame.**

   I want …

4. **Then write gratitude statements for these as if they are already true. Make this present tense. And if you can feel it and see it (in your mind) when writing this, it will amplify the power of these statements.**

   I am so happy and thankful now that… because….

You can decide to be more general or be super specific.

5. **How do you feel now? What did you notice from following this Journaling Guide?**

Take this to the next level: Do this every day!

Example:

1. **Write 5-10 things you are grateful for. Add why each thing is valuable to you by adding 'because' to deepen the gratitude.**

   I am grateful for living in a peaceful place because that makes me feel safe and helps me sleep peacefully at night. It makes me feel like I am truly fortunate to be raising my children in a place where there is peace.

   I am grateful for my children being healthy because seeing them grow is so precious.

   I am grateful that I do work I truly love because it feeds my soul and mostly it doesn't feel like work at all.

   I am grateful for this coffee mug because it reminds me of our holiday in Greece.

I am grateful for having clean running water in my tap because that is life-giving.

2. **Then write at least 5 statements starting with the words: I love my life because...**

   I love my life because I make time to journal.

   I love my life because I live in a peaceful part of the world.

   I love my life because I have access to learning every day and it is fun for me.

   I love my life because I have so many choices daily.

   I love my life because I can go to a café to journal and it has music that makes me smile.

3. **What are at least 5 things you want to happen / experience / improve in the next little while?**

   I want to feel calmer. I want really strong core muscles. I want to get a promotion and a pay rise. I want to invite my mum on a spa trip. I want to have a deeper connection with my partner.

4. **Then write gratitude statements for these as if they are already true.**

   I am so happy and thankful now that I feel calmer because I find myself being more present in my relationships.

   I am so happy and thankful now that I have strong core muscles because I have much more energy to play and work.

I am so happy and thankful now that I am on a spa trip with my mum because treating her to something like this is the best feeling.

I am so happy and thankful now that I got the promotion and a healthy pay rise because I feel acknowledged for all that I give to work and the extra money makes life a lot more fun.

5. **How do you feel now? What did you notice from following this Journaling Guide?**

   I feel great. Actually, I am surprised how fun this was. Makes me appreciate how many good things are in my life, and I really like feeling gratitude also for things I want for the future. It feels a lot better feeling gratitude than impatience.

Let one wonderful thought infect everything else in your day

■ ■ ■

23

When you want to stop holding back and start living your dreams

Are you clear about your dreams? If failure didn't exist, what would you go for?

This Journaling Guide is for a day when you are ready to dive into what it is you really want. You will not get to live a life of dreams unless you become conscious about what those dreams really are, and then start moving towards them.

In the busy day-to-day living, it can be easy to set the bar low. You might tell yourself: I will be happy if things just get a tiny bit better. But will you?

Why not aim for something truly fantastic? When we aim small, we tend to receive small. When we aim high, we might not achieve what we want immediately, but, in the stretch, we will grow and progress much more. And that can feel truly satisfying.

Anyone living an incredible life started with just having a dream. They then decided that dream was a vision. Something they could move towards. And then they started "moving".

Are you ready to activate your dream-muscles and momentum?

Let's journal.

What would you want to do, be and have if you knew you couldn't fail?

What would your personal life look like if you knew you could have what you truly wanted?

If it was truly better for everyone that you had what made you happy, what would you do, be, have?

If you feeling your best was truly the best for your employer / company what would you do, be, have?

If the universe gave you a window of 3 weeks where anything you initiated would be guaranteed success and massive momentum, what would you action?

Scan what you have written. What does it tell you about what you really want to be, have and do?

What fears or self-limiting thoughts came up as you journaled on these questions?

What will it take for you to make today the moment where you make these things happen? What moves / actions will you take today, so that the 'future you' gets to live her dreams? (It is easy to think we have a life-time to make

our dreams come true. But time does pass. And right now, is your most powerful moment)

What else will it take for you to live the life of your dreams now?

Example:

I will not give you an example here as I want you to have a truly blank canvas for this Journaling Guide. I will, however, encourage you to action whatever your answers were to the question of having 3 weeks where you had guaranteed momentum. Even if success isn't guaranteed look at how you can take some action straight away.

Journaling isn't enough if you want to live your dreams. Aligned action is required too and that might take some courage. But you can do it. Just take one step at a time and use the other Journaling Guides as additional support; for example, Guide 05 to believe more in yourself and Guide 20 to avoid procrastination.

If you have not exercised your dream muscles in a while, you might feel a little rusty as you journal through the questions. That is OK. Let the questions marinate in the back of your mind and return to this Guide a couple of weeks later.

Your power is always in the present moment

■ ■ ■

24

When you want to expand, upgrade and grow

Are you ready for an upgrade? To activate your courage? You can make incredible things happen when you are in a great state of mind.

This Journaling Guide is for when you are ready to flourish and expand. Maybe you will use it for your work, career or business. Maybe for your life overall, or for another specific part of your life, such as your health or relationship. Either way, this will help you grow.

The questions will also help you notice how you might have been keeping yourself (unconsciously) stuck in the status quo. Even when we don't like our status quo, it is familiar, and because we are used to our current reality, it often feels more comfortable than the unknown. Change requires us to do something different and our fear-driven mind might tell us that is scary.

If we are thinking the same thoughts we have been thinking for years and taking actions that are similar to those we have done in previous years, then it is not surprising if nothing much is changing or upgrading.

It is time to tap into your courage, up-level and become even more magnificent.

Let's journal.

What specifically do you want to expand / upgrade / grow?

Why do you want to expand / upgrade / grow in this area?

What do you believe would be different in your life if you really did expand and grow in this or those areas?

So, what is it that you really want?

What are you getting out of staying stuck? What do you not have to deal with by staying in your current reality?

What bold moves are you resisting taking? And why?

If you knew you would succeed or that it would pay off, what moves would you make now? (Moves might be investing in something, saying yes or no to something, starting something, letting go of something)

Imagine you had already upgraded or expanded in the area you wanted to. Write how great it (and you) would look, feel, sound, be:

Look at everything you have written. What are your reasons / excuses for not just taking the steps towards upgrading now? What do you notice about why you haven't made this upgrade or expansion yet?

What do you need to believe about yourself, others and the world to take those steps?

What will you decide and commit to now?

Example:

What specifically do you want to expand / upgrade / grow?

> *My career. A more senior role.*

Why do you want to expand / upgrade / grow in this area?

> *I have been in the same academic role for seven years. I am bored and demotivated.*

What do you believe would be different in your life if you really did expand and grow in this or those areas?

> *I would enjoy my work again. My passion would flow. I would find it easier to secure more funding for my research. I would be able to contribute more to the field because I would be seen to have more authority.*

So, what is it that you really want?

> *I want to love my work, contribute to the field and be respected as an important voice in the field.*

What are you getting out of staying stuck? What do you not have to deal with by staying in your current reality?

In this status quo I can hide and coast. When my children are ill or my dad's health issues flare up, I don't feel guilty for working less. The status quo is making me feel freer to be there for my family. And by not being in the limelight my research doesn't get scrutinised that much.

What bold moves are you resisting taking? And why?

I haven't gone boldly to the Head of Department to ask him to back my promotion and to share how it will benefit everyone. Instead I have been waiting and hoping they would eventually promote me without me having to really sell myself

If you knew you would succeed or that it would pay off, what moves would you make now?

I would create a business case for my promotion and confidently show the Head of Department that my promotion will benefit the research and the rest of the department.

Imagine you had already upgraded or expanded in the area you wanted to, write how great it (and you) would look, feel, sound, be:

I would walk into meetings with a new bounce in my step. I can see myself excitedly writing new grant applications and starting collaborations with industry and other departments. I can feel the bubbly happy energy inside.

Look at everything you have written. What are your reasons / excuses for not just taking the steps towards upgrading now? What do you notice about why you haven't made this upgrade or expansion yet?

Fear that I will not be able to be there for my family as much. Not wanting to sell myself. Fear of rejection and embarrassment in terms of work.

What do you need to believe about yourself, others and the world to take those steps?

I need to believe that:

- *A promotion will still allow me to be available to my family and their needs in a lot of ways.*
- *I am good enough for this and there is no embarrassment if I get told no.*

I can see now how I have just been waiting to be appointed and hoping it would land in my lap. But that is not showing any leadership.

What will you decide and commit to now?

I realised that I have been quite passive. I don't want it to be all about the promotion. I want it to be about the elevation of my research, adding more value to the field and therefore also to the department. I commit to speaking to the Head of Department this week and no matter what I will add more value to the field. It is about leading now; not waiting for a title change.

You weren't born to be lukewarm

■ ■ ■

25

When it is time to step into possibilities and believe big

This is such a fun and courage-activating Journaling Guide, that I think you will want to use it often. It will help you "play big" in the world in a really good-feeling kind of way.

When you meet a person, you get a sense of their energy and state of mind. Are they low-energy and draining to hang around or uplifting and inspiring? Which of those people are more likely to attract exciting opportunities?

It is rare that your negative friend has all kinds of wonderful things happen to them. Not because they aren't wonderful, but because of their energy frequency and the way they are interacting with the world at that moment. Our frequency is like a radio station tuned into a certain channel of opportunities. Good news is that our frequency isn't static and we can change it in any moment.

You probably already know the negative "what if" game. The one where you think about all the things that could go wrong. For example, if you want to go for a promotion you might think: What if I don't get the job, or what if the promotion means I will have less time with my children or what if I fail at it and so on. If you play the negative "what if" game for an extended period of time your frequency will turn towards more unattractive opportunities.

In this Journaling Guide we are playing a much better game: The "what if possibilities" game. I want you to think about what could go "right". For example, if we stay with the example of wanting the promotion, you might think: What if this would make me love my job even more, and what if that means I have more patience and energy for my children, and what if this promotion would have me spend more time at my best and therefore I would actually be working less hard and... and... and …

When we allow ourselves to activate the energy of possibilities and we enjoy staying with that vibe without needing immediate proof that results are coming, it becomes easier to attract great opportunities.

Allow your excitement to build and hold faith that the possibility-activation will magnetise great things to you. Maybe exactly what you imagined, or maybe something even better.

Let's journal.

Where have you been "playing small" in your work?

How do you know that you could "play bigger", go for more opportunities and set your sight on more exciting possibilities?

Where and how would you like to "play bigger"?

Let's play the "what if possibilities" game. What could go right / brilliant / better than you could imagine if you started "playing big"? (Don't' censor. Just be playful and write)

What if… and… what if… and… what if…

Now let's go even bigger. Allow your mind to let go of any restrictions and go all in on imagining the utmost expansive and delicious scenarios / outcomes / possibilities.

To help you, you can use these prompts:

It would be totally magical and wonderful if ….

It would be absolutely amazing and crazy if ….

And… and.. and…

While you are in the energy of possibilities I want you to anchor in new beliefs and schedule aligned actions. What do you want to keep telling yourself? And what next steps do you want to initiate this week?

Example:

Where have you been playing small in your life and work?

> *I have been busy doing all the tasks, attending meetings and replying to all the incoming emails. In all areas of my life, I have been so busy that I have*

mostly been trying not to drown in all the day to day stuff.

How do you know that you could play bigger, go for more opportunities and set your sight on more exciting possibilities?

Because I look at what we are doing in the business and feel frustrated and I can feel I have ideas of how to make everything better.

Where and how would you like to play bigger in your life and work? And why?

I would like to shape the future of our region. I love our company purpose and our brand, and I would like to shape more of our strategy and vision because I believe I have something very important to add.

Let's play the "what if possibilities" game. What could go right / brilliant / better than you could imagine if you started "playing big"? Don't' censor. Just be playful and write:

What if I cancelled a day of meetings and captured all my creative thoughts about how to elevate our region? And what if I came out of that day so inspired that I felt the courage to say no to some of the less important things, we are working on? And what if everyone around me was so grateful that I took the lead on the vision and everyone felt so relieved that we cancelled several time-wasting projects? This is making me feel excited.

Now let's go even bigger. Allow your mind to let go of any restrictions and go all in on imagining the utmost expansive and delicious scenarios / outcomes / possibilities.

It would be totally amazing if I spent 50% of my time being visionary and strategic and if I used my people skills to ignite the passion there is in my team and in the whole region. It would be absolutely magical if my energy became so infectious that it felt like we were back to the early days when the business was all new. And what if I could have so much fun, that I would have much more energy, and my boyfriend would feel it too, and he would also become inspired to uplift his career.

While you are in the energy of possibilities I want you to anchor in new beliefs and schedule aligned actions. What do you want to keep telling yourself? And what next steps do you want to initiate this week?

I am ready to be visionary and strategic and I can make the space and time for this. When I spend more time on how to make the longer-term vision come to life, I am helping everyone in the business. I will block Thursday from 11am and kindly decline all meeting invitations. I am starting this new momentum this week.

Activate possibilities by giving your imagination and excitement free rein to play

■ ■ ■

DIALOGUE JOURNALING

Take your journaling to a new level

If you are ready to journal without structured questions and take your journaling to a whole new level, I want to introduce you to Dialogue Journaling.

Dialogue Journaling is a magical and profound way to self-coach.

More than 16 years of coaching high performers, leaders and business owners has taught me that what makes thinking really tricky is that we muddle all our thoughts together. All our different thoughts swirl in the same space in our mind.

We might have a super helpful thought, then seven unhelpful thoughts, back to two helpful ones, then a neutral one and then another five unhelpful ones. All mixed together, it is almost impossible to find rhyme or reason in that. We convince ourselves that we need to think more to get clarity, and then round we go in the same thinking loops.

Dialogue Journaling is a method that helps you separate and organise your thoughts. In fact, it will help you cultivate the wisest voice inside of you. This form of journaling will catapult your ability to really coach and support yourself. You may even be able to access insights that are beyond anything you thought you knew.

Dialogue journaling is written as a film or play script. It can be a dialogue between you and a book you want to write, you and your body, you and a project or, my favourite, between you and the divine / higher self. If the word divine doesn't work for you, call it wisdom or higher self.

Let me show you a few examples of Dialogue Journaling, and then I will give you some more tips on how to get started.

Let your heart ask
the questions

Let your mind get
still

Let your body
receive the answers

■ ■ ■

Examples of Dialogue Journaling

With your body

Sara: Hello body and specifically sore shoulder. How do I make you better?

Body: You start by making me a priority. Don't think of how you can use me. Think of how you can make me more valuable.

Sara: I guess that's different.

Body: Of course, it is. When you just want to use me, you think of how you can just keep going, pushing yourself a little further by focusing on something outside of you, that you think needs to get done. When you are looking to make me more valuable, you tune into me daily and then you will notice what I need.

Sara: I am pretty sure I know what you need.

Body: That is very likely. But knowledge isn't worth much if you ignore it.

Sara: Haha. True that. Hmmm... So, I guess it is more about making time for it.

Body: I have heard you tell yourself the story many times that you don't have enough time to exercise and enough time to stretch. But that is totally missing the point.

Sara: What is the point?

Body: Without me you are nothing.

Sara: True...

Body: And when I work optimally, you are so much more powerful, you feel much better, and yes, I will actually save you time. I know you are obsessed with how much time anything takes.

Sara: It sounds like worrying about the time it takes to look after you is the wrong focus.

Body: Yes. But I don't think you have fully gotten it yet. Intellectually you get it. But you are so caught up in this fear-world where time is a zero-sum game. You will gain more energy when I am working optimally. That equals time back. That equals potency in all your actions. That equals more of a possibility mindset that will make things more possible.

Sara: OK. So, I think it is time to ask not what I can fit in to make you better, rather how can I do everything in my power to make you work optimally.

Body: Yes. That would be great. But don't try to go from 0-100 in one moment. Because this is like a muscle you need to train. Commit to something new now and then layer on top of it.

Sara: That makes sense. Do you have a preference for what I start with?

With a project or a part of your business

(The Female Inner Power Club – FIPC – is an online program)

Noomi: Hello Female Inner Power Club

FIPC: Hello. I am glad you are talking to me instead of just thinking about me.

Noomi: I guess I do think about you and forget to talk to you. I definitely get in my head a lot. I do a lot of thinking and I don't always follow through.

FIPC: I am glad you see that. I like it when you take action. When you are in your female inner power, and you are role modelling what you teach. Thinking is great but not when it is the same thoughts over and over again.

Noomi: I know what you mean. What is it you wish I would ask you or take action on?

FIPC: First up I wish you would stop questioning my worth. Each time you are unsure of my value, I get really heavy and tired, and then my value decreases. I become less attractive to new potential members. I am a worthy creation. I am incredibly powerful.

Noomi: I often question your power because I see you as an extension of me, so it depends on how I feel about myself on any given day.

FIPC: I am a creation that is separate from you. You might have created me, but I am not you. When you doubt my power, you can ask me to remind you of how I transform the lives of members. You can also ask me how I can become more valuable to the world.

With divine / higher self

Hannah: I don't know if I can focus today. And I want to. There are lots of things to do. So many things.

Divine: You are speaking from lack. Lack of time. And lack of faith in yourself. Not believing you can focus. Start with acknowledging your amazingness.

Hannah: OK that's actually kind of annoying. I get what you are saying but I know myself. On days without deadlines and with lots of things that need to get done but don't have to get done today, it's so easy to spend lots of time doing... actually I don't know what... but various procrastination activities that don't leave me satisfied in any way. And that aren't really about resting either.

So yes, perhaps my question is coming from lack – or perhaps this is coming from the experience of knowing myself.

Divine: I get it. And still... I want you to breathe. Breathe again. That's better. Breathe more. Land in your body. You were in your head. Breathe.

Hannah: OK I am breathing but where is the gold nugget. Help me please. And quick please.

Divine: All in good time my child. Now breathe again. Let's see how I can best speak to you in a way that will shift the energy in your body. Today it will be helpful to organise the list. But not looking at a list for the whole day. Because when you add that many things you will think – that isn't possible. It is better for you to just add the tasks for the next hour or so. And